MW01146067

Do-It-Yourself Magnetic Therapy

By Richard Tamir

Contents

Introduction

I am an informal scientific thinker – I look for proof, and don't generally follow trends. What that means is that I investigate new ideas with an open mind, but trust only my own experience when faced with new concepts. There are a lot of accepted ideas I don't believe, and a number of unusual ideas that I have experienced and believe in. That is the reason for writing this book.

A few years ago, I had an unusual experience: without any pre-conceived expectations, I tried using a magnet to help a painful condition in my hand. (The full description is in Chapter 1.) To my amazement, it worked. And not only did it work, the results were faster and better than typical medical treatments. The magnets were given to me by a consulting client, an engineering firm, with no suggestion of health treatment. They were simply examples of the powerful new neodymium "super-magnets", and were astonishingly powerful. These magnets have only been available since the 1990s, thanks to new manufacturing processes. My first health experiment occurred in 2002, and I have been experimenting with neodymium magnets ever since.

I have seen some amazing results, both in me and in others. I have also observed some conditions that did not improve – but no health conditions that have worsened. I don't pretend to be a doctor, a physicist or a scientific researcher. But I do have an inquisitiveand logical mind, like many people, and believe that anyone has the right to investigatenew ideas for themselves and tell others about it.

This book is my report to you on my investigations, including:

1. the experiments that were done;
2. the specific results for each;
3. experimental controls that made the experiment believable and repeatable;
4. how each magnetic device was made, and where I purchased the necessary materials; and
5. finally, how you can do the same experiment yourselves at low cost?

As a former high-tech product manager / consultant / attorney, my training was to keep all technology details secret – that's how to protect a product. But neodymium magnetsare not a secret anymore, and simply putting them on a painful muscle, either with tape ora small pad, is not protected by patent or trademark. And there's no reason you can't putthese magnets on an elastic knee bandage yourself at a cost of $15, instead of paying up to $130 for an identical manufactured product from the Internet.

So this book will follow a different principle: "full information disclosure". What doesthis mean for you, the reader? Simply that you will have all the data needed to build yourown magnetic therapy devices – cheap, fast and effective. For most of these designs, youcan save 75% or more of the price of devices sold on the internet.

Now, for the first time, you have a book that "tells all" about magnetic therapy – what todo, where to buy materials, how much to pay, etc. From my perspective, it's the best wayto bring magnetic therapy to the largest number of people. And with the detail providedfrom my own past experiments, you can try them out for yourself.

Magnetic therapy is real and is highly effective. It doesn't depend on belief – it's a physical phenomenon, as yet unexplained by medical science, that has brought relief tomillions of people. Try it out yourself, using the low-cost designs provided here. Youmay find that your life has a lot less pain in it from aging, muscular strains, over-exertionor other everyday occurrences.

A NOTE ABOUT MAGNETIC HEALTH PRODUCTS ON THE INTERNET:

There are many companies on the Internet selling magnetic bracelets, knee braces andother devices.

- "Devices": this is a poor word to use, but probably the best available. What dowe mean by a "device"? It's not a machine, at least not in this book. Usually, itwill be an elastic bandage that fits around the arm, leg, knee, etc. with magnetsattached to it. That's the kind of device we're talking about.

In most cases, the Internet magnetic health devices are highly overpriced. Once company, for example, offer a magnetic knee brace with standard-strength magnets for

$39.95 – but with 6 neodymium "super-magnets" added, the price went to $131.50 (2005prices). How much does one of these super-magnets cost? At most, the retail price is about $1.00; in quantities of 5,000 – 10,000 magnets, the price is about $0.15 each – fifteen cents! That's a 1600% markup (or 100,000% at manufacturer volume quantities)to the Internet customer for each neodymium magnet.

- NOTE: The neodymium super-magnets discussed here have a force of 12,500 Gauss (see Chapter 1 for definition), and are the same model described as "high-energy, research-grade magnets' at one Internet website for their top-of-the-linemagnetic health products.

To see the variety of products available, as well as the prices charges, please refer to thetable at the end of this Introduction. Many, if not most, of the products that are listed inthat table can be made at home – at low cost and with little effort, using standard materials from local drugstores or athletic stores, plus magnets purchased from an online supplier.

In Appendix A, you'll see where to buy your own super-magnets and other magnetic materials, to build your own super-magnet knee brace at very low cost. (My cost was under $25.00.) If you want to see the large variety of designs on the market, Appendix C provides websites of companies selling magnetic health devices online. Most of theseyou can duplicate at much lower cost, using standard athletic braces (elastic bandages forknee, elbow, leg, etc.) from the drugstore.

- Note: Prices in this book for magnetic materials will be retail prices. Lower prices are possible, but manufacturing quantities of 5,000+ magnets are not realistic for most readers. Besides, you'll have to go to China to find them.

I make no medical recommendations here. What you will read is the truth of what I experienced, and how you can make the same experiments yourself. All the experiencesreported are true, and to that I will swear in any court. The opinions you will read are my own (unless specifically attributed to another source), developed through 5 years of experimentation.

Please enjoy this book, and continue experimenting on your own. If you find that one ofthese designs helps improve your health, use it with our blessing. If you want to tell usabout your own experiences, an email to oleh77@yahoo.com would be great.

HANDLING SUPER-MAGNETS

If you haven't handled super-magnets before, please read this section before you do.These magnets are very strong, and can sometimes catch you by surprise.

1. Super-magnets will tend to jump up to attach themselves to other magnets. If thefingers of an elderly or very young person are in the

way, they could be pinchedpainfully.
Therefore, try to keep magnets separated
from each other.

2. It is nearly impossible to pull these magnets
    apart, especially in the 12,500 Gaussmodel.
    The solution is to slide them apart, moving
    the top magnet sideways untilit protrudes
    over the next one – and then it can be pried
    up by the edge with a little strength and good
    grip.

3. To enable the above sliding motion, super-
    magnets should be kept clean so thattheir
    surface has low friction. Even colored stick-
    on paper dots can increase thisfriction.
    Therefore, if your hand strength is not very
    high, I suggest " tagging" only a few super-
    magnets with colored dots and use these as a
    reference to determine the polarity of other
    magnets. How to do this? Simply pass the
    magnetyou are working with over the color-
    coded magnet – if the magnets attract, the
    magnet faces have the same polarity. This
    will tell you which side should be placed
    touching the skin, or away from the body. If
    the magnets repel each other,then flip the
    magnet you are working with onto the other
    side.

4. If you don't have much hand strength at all,
    magnets can be kept separate byletting
    them attach to an iron or steel surface – the
    side of a refrigerator, for example. Then
    they can be slid to the corner of the
    refrigerator, where they willbe easy to
    remove.

5. Some super-magnets are shipped with
    plastic separators between them, to make
    working with them easier. You may wish to

continue using the separators.

6. If you tape magnets to your skin with a red-dot sticker on the outside, it's likely that the colored surface of the sticker will come off with the tape. Simply put another sticker on top of the remaining paper surface; if this happens frequently,

you can periodically remove the paper remnants with a paper towel and a bit of benzene or other petroleum-distillate solvent. (Wear protective gloves so that the solvent will not damage your skin, and work in a well-ventilated place to avoid inhaling fumes.) With more experience, you will find that you only need to put red-dot indicators on a few reference magnets and leave the "working magnets" clean for easy sliding off magnet stacks.

7. **Never bring super-magnets close to the following objects – their stored data will be erased, and they will be unusable:**
   a. **Floppy computer disks (but CDs are OK);**
   b. **Credit cards, or your wallet in general;**
   c. **Any airline/bus/train tickets that have a magnetic stripe on the back;**
   d. **Any electronic devices that seem to behave strangely when brought near the magnets. Generally, cellphones are not affected.**
   e. **Most important, keep these magnets away from computer or television screens. They will make the colors change on the screen, and this will sometimes remain. Newer screens have a de-gaussing circuit built in that will repair this when the screen is turned off and on, but older screens do not.**

   i. **DE-GAUSSING TV OR COMPUTER SCREENS:** bring a single magnet close to the screen slowly until you see the discoloration change, then move the magnet in circles as you slowly move it away from the screen. This is often effective, but may need repetition.

IMPORTANT MEDICAL NOTE:

ANYONE WHO IS USING A PACEMAKER OR OTHER ELECTRICAL OR ELECTRONIC MEDICAL DEVICE MUST KEEP SUPER-MAGNETS AT LEAST 18"AWAY FROM THOSE DEVICES. MAGNETIC FIELDS CAN INTERFERE WITH THEIR OPERATION.

SAFETY OF SUPER-MAGNETS IN HEALTH THERAPY:

TO MY KNOWLEDGE, INCLUDING RESULTS OF EXTENSIVE INTERNET RESEARCH, THERE ARE NO KNOWN REPORTS OF DAMAGE CAUSED BY USEOF MAGNETS ON THE HUMAN BODY.

TO THE CONTRARY: AN M.R.I. ("Magnetic Resonance Imaging") MACHINE – USED IN HOSPITALS TO VIEW THE BODY'S INTERIOR – CREATES A MAGNETIC FORCE FAR HIGHER THAN THOSE DISCUSSED IN THIS BOOK.

READY-MADE MAGNETIC THERAPY DEVICES:

For reference purposes, below are the prices that were charged in 2005 for variousmagnetic therapy devices displayed on the internet.

With this book, you can make your own devices for a small fraction of these prices, andcan make devices that can be used in many different areas of the body. Instead of spending $300-$500, you may find that $50 of materials are all you need to make yourown magnetic therapy devices.

Industry Comparison Of Magnetic Health Products
(as of January 2006)

Company	Knee Support	Elbow	Wrist Wrap	Wrist Support	Ankle Support	Calf Support	Thigh Support	Shoulder Support	Lower Back	TOTAL - FULL LINE
COMPANY A standard magnets	$39.95	$24.95	$19.95	$28.96	$27.95	$44.95	$49.96	$105.95	$69.95	$412.55
	$73.50	$43.00	$49.00	$29.60	$50.00	$75.00	$89.00	$174.00	$143.50	$724.50
COMPANY A standard + neodymium	$118.00	$67.50								NdFeB Increase = 76% Minimum
	$131.50									
	$72.00	$67.00	$49.00			$72.00		$174.00	$48.00	
	$129.00	$43.00							$79.00	
COMPANY B									$142.00	
COMPANY C	$31.99	$22.99	$11.99		$19.99				$39.99	
COMPANY D	$16.95	$12.95	$14.95	$15.95			$15.95	$129.95	$29.95	$239.65
	$39.95	$22.57	$22.16	$33.19	$18.50	$28.95	$37.95	$29.00	$89.61	$321.79
	$42.95	$31.39		$12.50	$32.63				$59.95	
			$13.95	$21.50					$36.95	
COMPANY E			$23.95							
	$49.95	$49.95	$34.95		$17.95				$74.95	
	$24.95	$34.95	$14.95		$39.95				$29.95	
COMPANY F			$19.95							
	$69.95	$69.95	$26.95		$43.95		$47.95	$74.95		
COMPANY G			$26.95							
COMPANY H		$41.50	$34.95	$24.95	$47.95					
AVERAGE PRICE	$64.74	$37.20	$27.29	$23.58	$30.65	$54.73	$48.16	$114.64	$70.32	

Chapter 1 – How It All Started

In the spring and summer of 2002, I was working as a business consultant. My age was 57 and my health was excellent, yet somehow I developed a very painful condition at the base of my right thumb. The bottom thumb joint started getting painful and increased to the point that I couldn't use it at all without serious pain.

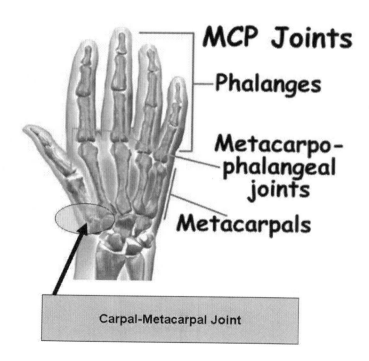

ANATOMY OF RIGHT HAND, SHOWING

THUMB JOINT AFFECTED

Naturally, I consulted a doctor and x-rays were taken. The condition was identified as osteoarthritis, and cause was attributed to the aging process. The doctor could easily see the condition and pointed it out to me on the x-rays. [1] [2]

The diagnosis was clear, and the prognosis was continued worsening and increasing pain. The only medical remedy was to take anti-inflammatory painkillers (NSAIDs), such as

----

[1] The National Institutes of Health describes osteoarthritis as follows: "Osteoarthritis is the most common joint disorder. The chronic disease causes the cushioning (cartilage) between the bone joints to wear away, leading to pain and stiffness. It can also cause new pieces of bone, called bone spurs, to grow around the joints."

[2] For further information: http://www.nlm.nih.gov/medlineplus/ency/article/000423.htm

Advil®. I was upset about the lack of a solution, probably because "I wasn't old" – atleast, not in my own mind.

A few weeks after that medical diagnosis, I had a thought: many people had told me thatmagnets were effective against this type of condition, so why not try it out? The conceptsounded ridiculous to me, since I had never heard an explanation of why magnets shouldbe effective. But it just happened that I had two tiny "super-magnets" that a consulting clients had given to me earlier that summer. I had nothing to lose, so I tried out the magnets.

- What are super-magnets? These are a new kind of magnet made from neodymium, a rare earth on the Periodic Table of Elements (element #60). The resulting super-magnets are used in many of today's computers and high-tech devices.[3]

I had 2 tiny neodymium magnets. [Officially, these are also called NdFeB magnets because they contain Neodymium + Iron + Boron.] My consulting client used themsimply to keep the door closed on their metal cabinets for public information kiosks. Personally, I found the little magnets fascinating because they were so strong. *"Believe ItOr Not" – a neodymium magnet can lift up to 1300 times its weight!*

THE EXPERIMENT

Here's the experiment I tried:
   1. I took a simple cotton sock and placed it over

   my right hand;
2. The 2 magnets were taped, touching each other, onto the sock directly over the painful joint;
3. I slept with this "hand sock" overnight.

I didn't notice much change the next morning – in fact, I probably forgot about the wholething. But I put on the device the next night, too. And sometime in the middle of the following day I realized something – my joint had no pain! It had absolutely no pain, noteven a little. In fact, the joint felt so normal that I didn't even realize the experiment was a success until the middle of that second day.

Beyond that, I can report today – 5 years later – that this joint has never had pain since. The condition went away permanently after 2 nights of magnetic treatment. However, don't be misled: I have also conducted other experiments, nearly all of them successful, using neodymium magnets – but only a few have had permanent pain relief. Most have

---

[3] To see patents in this area, go to http://www.uspto.gov/patft/index.html. To see the sintering process patents, do a Quick Search on "Neodymium + Sinter", then add "Magnet" after the first results screen. To see the wide variety of neodymium magneticdevice patents, just search on "Neodymium + Magnet".

had medium-term success in removing pain, relaxing muscles, improving tendon or otherinjuries. These results were generally effective for at least a few weeks, and often longer.

A SLIGHTLY DIFFERENT EXPERIENCE:

Here's another experiment to be compared to these first results: about 2 years later, thesame joint on the other hand started having the same type of pain. I assumed that it wasthe same condition and used the same method. The results were apparently identical –the pain immediately disappeared – but on the left thumb joint it came back 1-2 months later. What was happening here? Why were these different results?

Eventually I remembered a key difference in the medical history of the 2 thumb joints. The right hand had no history of injury, and apparently was only experiencing the onset of age-related osteoarthritis. On the other hand (pun intended), the left thumb joint wasdislocated in 1974 when it was bent fully backward. Apparently, that dislocation left a permanent condition in the joint, which caused the pain to reappear. Now, a few years ofmagnetic treatments later, I can report that the left-hand joint pain does come back – b u t it comes back after longer and longer time intervals. Now, the time between painful periods is 3-4 months; at the beginning, it was 3-4 weeks.

MY REACTIONS AT THE TIME:

What did I think about this sudden turn-around, perhaps even "cure", of the osteoarthritic pain in my right thumb joint? I was amazed, I was stupefied – and I was intrigued. What could possibly explain this result? Such an outcome was unexpected and unexplained by accepted medical thinking. I expected that many doctors would not believe my story – which has turned out to be true in all cases except two (to be described in a later chapter).

So what should I do? I am not a doctor, although I have learned a lot of medical information informally from my family. My father was a pharmaceutical researcher, and my uncle was a doctor. My family's intellectual approach was to believe only what could be proven – and now I had a personal proof, although not medically documented, that there was a medical phenomenon to be investigated.

To me, there are 2 types of scientists:
1. "So-called scientists" – people with scientific training who apply the formal rules they have learned to all situations. When faced with facts that contradict or go beyond these rules, the "so-called scientist" doubts the source of the information and/or dismisses the story. For them, the rules of science forever remain unquestioned.
2. "True scientists" – when faced with facts that are outside the rules they have learned, they become intrigued and investigate the phenomenon further. They pursue the information until they have an explanation, or until the case is proven to be false. Often, they can't get to a final answer, but the pursuit has led them in interesting directions.

Sometimes, they develop major new theories from their unrelenting search for the truth.

Although not a scientist, I follow the "true science" approach – when the rules don'texplain a phenomenon, research further until there is an explanation. And if an explanation isn't found, at least record the unexpected event formally to establish theexistence of the unusual phenomenon.

So that's what I did, and that's what you'll be reading in this book: a personal but semi-formal research study of the health-related effects of magnets. You'll even learn about aseries of formal, fully-controlled experiments into the effects of super-magnets on the taste and quality of wine, done in cooperation with a major winery. (You'll also see howto make a simple magnetic device that greatly improves wine in under 2 days.)

So sit back and relax, and enjoy your reading. I think you'll find it interesting.

CHAPTER NOTES

MATERIALS USED:

If you go to https://www.allmagnetics.com/craft/ndfeb.htm on the Internet, you'll see 3 different packages of neodymium magnets – small, medium and large. The magnets Iused in the initial thumb-joint experiment were the size of the small magnets shown, which are 0.315" in diameter and 0.118" thick. However, mine were slightly more powerful – the ones on that webpage are 10,000 Gauss, and the ones I used were 12,500Gauss.

- The company shown has magnets of many different strengths, but these retail packages for $3.99 come only in 10,000 Gauss magnetic strength. Call to requestother strengths and specifications. Large-size, 12,500-Gauss neodymium magnetsranged from $.65 to $0.98 apiece, plus shipping. There is a minimum mail-orderamount, so read Appendix A, "Designs & Materials Used", to make up a complete order. (This will probably be a $50 - $100 total cost, for a lifetime of   therapeutic use.)

WHAT ARE GAUSS?

Well, here goes: "Gauss" is a scientific unit of magnetic force, coming from the name ofGerman scientist Karl Friedrich Gauss (1777-1855), a leading thinker in   both mathematics and astronomy. You're probably familiar with another scientist's name used as a physical label, Heinrich Rudolf Hertz. His name is used as a unit of frequencies
– such as, "You're listening to WXYZ, broadcasting on 108.5 MegaHertz".

When using magnets with the human body, a Gauss can be considered a measurement of the surface strength of a magnetic field.[4] It is a measurement per unit area – in other words, a 10,000 Gauss magnet is still 10,000 Gauss no matter how large it is. The total magnetic force will be larger with a magnet of greater mass, but the force per unit area –its Gauss rating – will be the same.

Gauss ratings are important to compare the strength of different magnets, and to know their depth of penetration into the human body. A low-Gauss magnet may dissipate its force only 1/4-inch from the skin, while a high-Gauss magnet will still have significant strength 2-3 inches from the surface.

---

[4] Formally speaking, a Gauss is a measurement of magnetic flux density. But "When dealing with exposure of non-ferromagnetic material such as animals or cells, Magnetic Flux Density and Magnetic Field Strength can be assumed to be equal." See a more scientific explanation, including this summary sentence, at http://www.electric-fields.bris.ac.uk/MagneticFieldStrength.htm

Chapter 2 – Simple Devices for Magnetic Therapy

A Personal Note:

When you read this book, with all its personal experiments to heal pain or injury, you may think that I'm a cripple or bed-ridden. I'm not!! Remember that these events cover a period of 5 years – how many pains have you had in that time?

MAGNETIC DEVICES:

Early in these experiments, I researched the Internet thoroughly for magnetic health products. What I found was good for the suppliers, but not for the customers. For nearly all companies, every product offered was for a single part of the body. That meant you had to buy a different magnetic brace[5] for every place you wanted to treat. That is very
expensive. (A few suppliers also offered magnetic pads that could be placed anywhere, but these were not featured prominently – you had to go looking for them.)

This chart shows all the products I could find in 2005, which part of the body they were meant for, and their prices:

Industry Comparison Of Magnetic Health Products
(as of January 2006)

Company	Knee Support	Elbow	Wrist Wrap	Wrist Support	Ankle Support	Calf Support	Thigh Support	Shoulder Support	Lower Back	TOTAL - FULL LINE
COMPANY A standard magnets	$39.95	$24.95	$19.95	$28.95	$27.95	$44.95	$49.95	$105.95	$69.95	$412.55
	$73.50	$43.00	$49.00	$29.50	$60.00	$73.00	$99.00	$174.00	$143.50	$724.50
COMPANY A standard + neodymium	$116.00	$67.50								NdFeB increase = 76% Minimum
	$131.50									
	$72.00	$67.00	$49.00			$72.00		$174.00	$48.00	
	$129.00	$43.00							$79.00	
COMPANY B									$142.00	
COMPANY C	$31.99	$22.99	$11.99		$19.99				$39.99	
COMPANY D	$19.95	$12.95	$14.95	$15.95			$15.95	$129.95	$29.95	$238.65
	$39.95	$22.57	$22.16	$33.10	$18.50	$28.95	$37.95	$29.00	$89.61	$321.79
	$42.95	$31.39		$12.50	$32.63				$59.95	
		$13.95		$21.50					$36.95	
COMPANY E		$23.95								
	$49.95	$49.95	$34.95		$17.95				$74.95	
	$24.95	$34.95	$14.95		$39.95				$29.95	
COMPANY F		$29.95			$19.95					
COMPANY G	$69.95	$69.95	$26.95		$48.95		$47.95	$74.95		
			$28.95							
COMPANY H		$41.50	$34.95	$24.95	$47.95					
AVERAGE PRICE	$64.74	$37.20	$27.29	$23.58	$30.85	$54.73	$48.16	$114.64	$70.32	

Notice the column on the far right: here, you can see the "Total – Full Line" price forbuying all available products from that company. The Average Price for each product

---

[5] Here, "brace" means elastic bandage cut to fit the knee / elbow / etc.

(for example, averaging all companies' product prices for a knee brace) can be seen alongthe bottom row.

If you look at Company A (the top 2 lines), you will see that it has 2 different productlines:
1. The "regular" magnetic product line, using older-style magnets with a 2,500-4,300 Gauss strength.
2. The "premium" magnetic product line, which adds 12,500-Gauss neodymium magnets to the regular variety, or replaces them entirely. In the case of their kneebrace, for example, there are 10 neodymium magnets in each brace.

But look at the prices difference: for 10 neodymium magnets instead of lower strength, the consumer must pay from $58 to $91 dollars more – for adding magnets that cost   a total of $7.00 - 10.00 at their retail price. And in large-volume manufacturer pricing, theycost a total of only $1.50 - $1.80 additional.

To me, there were 3 factors that I found disturbing:
1. The outrageous profits made by adding a few, low-cost neodymium magnets;
2. The business generated ($10 million annually for one company) simply because consumers did not know how about adding neodymium magnets to elastic kneebraces, or where to purchase the materials.
3. The universal push by all sellers for customers to buy product A for location A, plus another product B for location B, etc.,

etc.

In answering objections #1 and #2, I envisioned a better way to provide magnetic therapy to the greatest number of people – using a "full information" approach. With full knowledge of these products and their use, consumers could choose to buy or make their own magnetic therapy devices. These would be just as effective as the ready-made models, but cost less.

Regarding objection #3, I conceived of a different product approach, the "Comfort Pad" –a small-to-medium size cloth envelope with a sheet of many neodymium high-strength magnets sealed inside. (Think of it as a large eyeglass case holding a flat sheet of neodymium magnets.) This could be placed anywhere on the body and be kept in p l a c e by elastic braces, surgical paper tape, or by being fixed to a shirt or other piece o f clothing. I have since seen similar examples of this design approach – once with even the same name – on the Internet. It doesn't take a rocket scientist to figure this out, and it can save consumers the very high cost of buying different devices for each afflicted part of the body. (Note: building your own Comfort Pads is fully described and illustrated later in this chapter.)

Later, when I had a large area of muscular stiffness and pain, I went beyond the ComfortPad designs to create a "Magnetic Comfort Sheet" device. This is a larger, but simpler, version of the Comfort Pad, suitable for covering large areas of the body such as the upper back.

Here's how a Comfort Sheet is constructed:

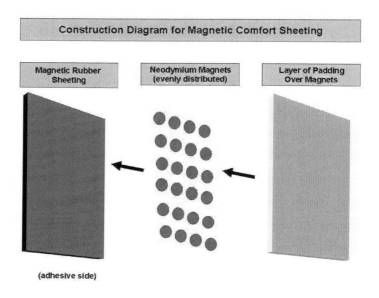

In summary, my experiments so far have involved 3 types of magnetic devices:
1. Simply taping the magnet over a painful point, using paper surgical tape
2. Using a "comfort pad" design for small to medium-size areas, or
3. Using a "comfort sheet" design for large areas.

1

I'm sure that there are many other designs possible. The ones that I used are described, diagramed and coasted to help you get started, since they have been very effective for me.

A NOTE ABOUT MAGNETIC POLARITY:

In western thinking, magnetic fields are viewed in a similar way to electric fields or electrical current. For example, a magnet taped to the skin without another magnet on theopposite side of the arm / leg / hand / etc., is called "open circuit". This is like a flashlight battery without anything connecting the positive and negative contacts, suggesting that nothing is happening without a "closed circuit". Very logical, we westerners.

In eastern thinking, however, magnetic fields are thought of as a force that either pullsenergy (also called Ki, chi or qi) out of the body, or moves it into the body. Energy can

Be bad (i.e., pain) or good (energy to raise our level of activity). In this approach, there isno need to "connect the poles" of a magnet by having an opposite-poled magnet nearby.

Here is an explanation of the eastern approach by James Chaffee, a practitioner ofTraditional Chinese Medicine and licensed acupuncturist:

- *"Magnetic force flows from the north pole (or south-seeking pole) to the southpole (or north-seeking pole). This flow of energy supplements and enhances the body's own intrinsic energies, called 'original or basal qi' in Chinese medicine. This type of energy allows the body to perform all of its daily functions and is required for people to live healthily.*
- *"Magnets also flow energy from the south pole (north-seeking pole) internally through the magnet up to the north pole. This type of flow helps expel or pull outpathogenic energies from the body to allow the body to recover."*

Examining both philosophies, there are 3 possible magnetic polarities:
1. "Inward force", where open-circuit energy ("qi") is forced inward;
2. "Outward force", where open-circuit energy is pulled outward;
3. "Closed circuit", where a magnetic field flows from a positive magnetic pole to a negative pole on another magnet.

In a later chapter, you will see how these 3 polarities were tested against each other in a double-blind research study with wines. There were clear differences in the results, which supported the "outward force" approach described in the next few paragraphs.

Throughout this book, my own health experiments always used "outward force" polarity.(This means the "red-dot side", as described next, will face away from the b o d y .)

Here's how to determine polarity and use it the same way as described in this book:

1. First, you need a standard compass for finding North. The compass needle has 2 points, one that faces North and one that faces South. Usually, they are colored differently – white for North and red for South. Note the color of the end that faces South – here, we'll call it the red point.

1. Standard Compass Facing Magnetic North

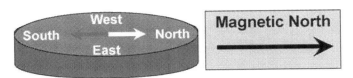

Note that the Red side of the needle faces South.

2. Face the compass toward one side of the magnet. The compass should be horizontal and the magnet should be vertical, so the compass needle is affected byonly one side of the magnet.

3.

2. Bring the Magnet Closer Until the *Red Needle Point* is Facing the Super-Magnet

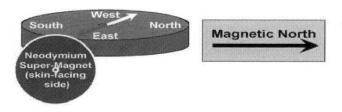

If the *Red Point* of the Needle Faces *Away from* the Super-Magnet, Turn the Magnet Around

4. As you bring the magnet toward the compass, the needle will swing to face it. Notice which end of the needle faces the magnet. If the red point faces themagnet, that is the "red-dot" side of the magnet and should always face awayfrom the body.
    a. If the white point faces the magnet, that is the side of the magnet thatshould be placed touching the body.

3. View of The Other Side of Magnet

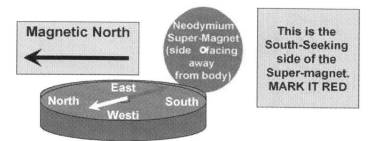

4. To assure the correct polarity, put a red marker on the side of the magnet that attracts the compass' red needle-point. (For my own experiments, I bought a set of red adhesive dots at Office Depot.)

5. Always put the red dot on the side facing away from the body. Comfort pads should also be covered with colored cloth, with the red side again facing away from the body.

6. Once you have determined the correct polarity for one magnet, it's easy to identify the polarity of all your magnets: if you have a pile of magnets all stucktogether, they all have the same polarity orientation.

A Note About Handling Super-Magnets:
SAFETY:

For those who haven't yet handled neodymium magnets, you're in for a surprise. Theyare stronger than you imagine – in fact, you probably can't separate 2 magnets of 12,500Gauss strength by pulling them apart. What's the trick? You have to slide them apart,but it still takes a bit of strength. For older folks, you may need to plan ahead – perhapsask a younger person, perhaps use a non-magnetic tool (plastic knife, etc.) to separate them.

Here are some safety tips to keep in mind:
1. Never let children play with these magnets. They can jump together and hurtsmall fingers.
2. When you are handling super-magnets, expect some unusual – and yes, funny – behavior at the beginning. When you have them close to each other, they willleap together when least expected – and when you pull 2 of them apart, someothers may jump into your hand unexpectedly.
3. When you're putting magnets in place, keep them separated by at least 5 to 6inches. The best method is to put them separately on a metal surface, such as theside of your

refrigerator, and slide each one to an edge when you want to remove it. They are relatively easy to remove from an edge.

4. When putting magnets together, one safe way is to hold the magnet you're adding on the inside of your fingers. Then bring the back of your hand toward the other magnets: the magnet in your hand will flip itself to the right polarity but be kept separated by the thickness of your fingers – this is not painful at all. Then slowly spread your fingers, and the magnets will attach in a gradual way without unexpected jumping.

5. You may want to show other people how strong these magnets are, possibly by letting them fly together at high speed. ***DON'T!*** There are 2 risks here:

    a. Someone's fingers may get in the way and get pinched (painful, but not very serious).

    b. The super-magnets can sometimes break from these high-speed collisions. Then you have 2 super-magnet fragments or more, which aren't very useful. But they are fun to play with, or to use for notes on the refrigerator.

CONVENIENCE:

1. Some suppliers ship super-magnets with plastic separators, to make them easier to pull apart. If you get some of these, don't throw them away. You'll be able to reuse them when handling stacks of neodymium magnets.

2. Later in this book, you'll read about taping super-magnets to various painful areas of the body for pain relief and more. These are the

best ways to do this:

a. Use paper surgical tape, available at any drugstore and not expensive at all.

b. Rip off sections of the tape beforehand, attaching them to the edge of a table. Each section should be at least 6 inches long.

c. Slide one super-magnet off the supply stack and check its polarity. Remember: always red-side away from the body.

d. Stick the red-side of the magnet to the tape at its midpoint. Do this for only 1 tape strip at a time, or you'll have a mess with all the tape strips swinging together and attaching to each other.

e. Take the tape strip with magnet, place the magnet on the center of the painful area, and then apply the tape to your skin.

f. It's better to change tape strips before showering, even though they will keep their stickiness. Why? Because before showering, the full strip and adhesive will come off your skin, leaving no residue. After getting wet and drying out, the tape will leave an adhesive residue on your skin which requires a solvent to remove.

g. If you're going to place a number of magnet in a small area, take care that the magnets don't jump together, either

    i. When you're applying them,

or

    ii.   After being taped to the skin.

h. If your points of pain are close together, you may want to apply tape allthe way around the arm, leg, knee, hand, etc. Without this extra-strengthtaping, the magnets can lift away from the skin and attach to each other. That's not necessarily bad, it just means that one locations has double-strength therapy, but the other location has none.

SUMMARY: THREE TYPES OF MAGNETIC DEVICES

SIMPLEST: TAPING MAGNETS TO YOUR SKIN

This is simply what the description reads: take a magnet and tape it to your skin, directlyabove the point of pain, injury, swelling, bruising, etc. Most important: make sure thatthe "red-dot side" (or whatever mark you're using) is facing away from the body.

If you have enough magnets available, you can tape a small stack of 2 or 3 magnets overthe painful location. When I used magnets this way, I have used up to 3 magnetstogether. In one situation, I wore 3 magnets on the top of a swollen and painful toe joint,and another 3 on the bottom while I was sleeping. In the morning there was major improvement – all swelling and pain had disappeared. These were changes that could beseen by anyone and measured or photographed. (See further discussion under "Hallux Valgus", below.)

EASIEST TO MAKE: MAGNETIC COMFORT SHEETING

In some cases, a point-specific approach (taping magnets to the body) or a small-area approach (using a Comfort Pad) are not sufficient. Muscle pain across the broad area of the upper back from the trapezius muscle, for example, needs a different solution.

In this case, try using the "Magnetic Comfort Sheeting" device. This is made from 2 magnetic materials, plus padding available at your supermarket:

1. SUPER-MAGNETS: A large number (about 25) of neodymium magnets, tested and marked for proper polarity;

2. MAGNETIC RUBBER SHEETING: A large piece (at least 10" by 15") of magnetized rubber sheeting. This is the industrial material used for magnetic business cards that people have on their refrigerator, but with the following differences:

   a. It is thinner – .020" instead of the .030" or thicker versions used for business card printing;

   b. It is supplied in rolls 24 inches wide and 10 feet long;

   c. In the preferred approach, one side should have contact adhesive on it and be covered with a removable paper layer.

3. PADDING MATERIAL: A roll of kitchen wipes made of dense non-woven material, about 10.5" x 14.5" for each sheet. Since the

sheets are attached to eachother lengthwise, but can be easily pulled apart using perforations, this is ideal forboth large- and small-area use. The material is about 1/16" thick, made of pressed, non-woven artificial fiber.

    a. (Note: Some of these products are impregnated with cleaning chemicalssuch as chlorine. Do not use these products, since they will seriously irritate the skin.)

    b. Where I live, a roll of 30 perforated wipes costs about $5.00 – that's a length of about 12 yards X 10.5" wide, or an area of about 32 square feet.

    c. In the U.S., these are probably easily found in your supermarket kitchen supplies section. If not, feel free to improvise: any clean, soft and thick wipe material will do – obviously, unused! Cotton wipes or even dishtowels can also be used – in fact, the cotton may be more comfortable when touching your skin, since it will absorb sweat.

DIRECTIONS FOR ASSEMBLING LARGE-AREA MAGNETIC SHEETING:

    1. From the roll of magnetic rubber sheeting (see ordering information in Appendix A), cut a piece that is slightly larger than the area of muscular stiffness. For the trapezius muscles, I used the full area of the 10.5" x 14.5"padding and cut the magnetized rubber sheeting to fit the back and go over myshoulder. Round all

corners to avoid any pain where touching the skin. (A strong pair of scissors or shears can cut this material. You can use a razor-knife and straight-edge ruler for long cuts.)

    a. NOTE: Do not yet remove the paper backing on the adhesive side.

2. Make sure that all the super-magnets (probably 25 or more for a sheet this large) have polarity stickers on the side to be placed away from the body, as described above.
3. Attach the magnets to the adhesive side of the rubber sheeting, evenlydistributed. The red-dot side should be touching the adhesive.
4. Apply the sheet of padding over the magnets, pushing it down to make contact with the adhesive. Trim all edges for smoothness and comfort.
5. Wear the Comfort Sheet by placing in the correct position over a piece of clothing such as a T-shirt, the fix the Comfort Sheet in place with small magnets on the other side of the T-shirt. This will prevent the Comfort Sheetfrom slipping.

If you look ahead to the next section, you'll see that the Comfort Sheeting is a larger andsimpler version of the magnetic "Comfort Pads" described below. It is easy to make, canlessen pain over large areas, and requires few materials.

CONVENIENT TO USE: MAGNETIC COMFORT PADS

Here's what a Comfort Pad looks like, showing how you can   make   one:

Comfort Pads – Sizes & Layouts

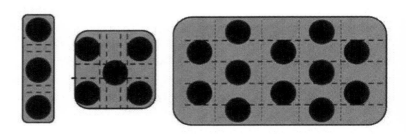

Comfort Pads – Cross-Section View

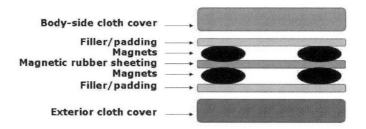

Body-side cloth cover

Filler/padding
Magnets
Magnetic rubber sheeting
Magnets
Filler/padding

Exterior cloth cover

The Magnetic Comfort Pad includes an absorbent cloth envelope, similar to an eyeglass case design, to allow it to be worn comfortably and conveniently. (If you're lucky, you may find an actual cloth eyeglass case that fits your needs in terms of size and padding.) Inside, place a cut-to-size magnetic sheet with neodymium magnets placed on its surface; apply a layer of padding between the magnets and the skin-side exterior for comfort.

Often, people make a double-layered magnetic sheet for the Comfort Pad, which brings relief sooner and penetrates deeper. Before sealing the Comfort Pad, always mark the correct polarity both on the internal magnetic sheeting and on the exterior. My approach was to use red cotton canvas for the side facing away from the body, and green cotton canvas for the side touching the body. That way there could be no mistaking the correct polarity, once the "red side away from skin" rule is learned.

Important Note about Spinal & Stomach Polarity:

There are two areas of the body where polarity rules are reversed:

1. The spine: within 2 – 3 inches of the spine, magnets should be placed with the red side touching the skin. I found this independently in my own experiments, and have since seen it repeated at various magnetic therapy websites.
2. The stomach: Although I have no experimental experience here, I am told that the same reverse-polarity

applies to the stomach area when trying to stop heartburn. I have no further information on this matter.

It is easy to know if the magnetic polarity should be changed: the location simply hurts more when you apply the magnetic device. Take the device off, reverse it and try it again. If the pain decreases, then you have found the right polarity. [If the pain worsens with both polarities, which I've never heard of, simply don't use a magnetic device there.] And don't worry that you won't feel a difference, or how long it might take: the difference is noticeable immediately, based on tests I've conducted using magnetic insoles. In the very first step after reversing my insoles, the pain level changed significantly. With the red-dot side under my soles and facing down to the ground, the pain in my feet was significantly less.

The following diagram shows how I used these various devices for pain in different areasof the body:

Comfort Pads: Sizes & Locations Used

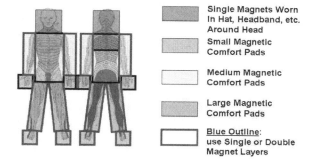

	Single Magnets Worn In Hat, Headband, etc. Around Head
	Small Magnetic Comfort Pads
	Medium Magnetic Comfort Pads
	Large Magnetic Comfort Pads
	Blue Outline: use Single or Double Magnet Layers

COMING ATTRACTIONS:

For the curious, here is an early look at my design for magnetic insoles:

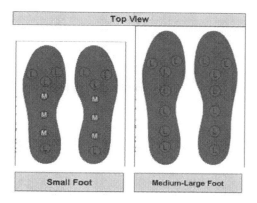

A later chapter will have full details on how to build

your own magnetic insoles in under30 minutes, and for less than $20 a pair.

Chapter 3 - Experiments for Discomfort, Pain or Injury

In this chapter, I will report on experiments with super-magnets from 2002-2007. In eachseparate experiment, the following information will be provided:

- **The nature of the condition**
- **The magnetic treatment method**
- **The results of the treatment**
- **Suggestions for general use**

Results of Magnetic Therapy Experiments:

Painful Muscle Cramps – Calf muscles

- **The nature of the condition**

I often get cramps in my calf muscles. I have tried stretching and exercise with some temporary effectiveness, and boron mineral supplements (no apparent effect after 1 year).Comfort Pads, however, have given me almost immediate relief, which is generally complete and lasts for a few days to a week.

The muscles involved can be seen in this anatomy drawing:

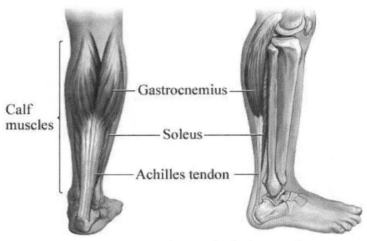

Anatomical picture of
lower leg muscles

The major muscles of the upper calf (gastrocnemius,
above) were in continual pain fromtightness or
cramping, causing serious discomfort.

First magnetic treatment method – COMFORT PAD:

My initial experiment was to take a comfort pad and place it inside an elastic knee brace, such as the one shown below:

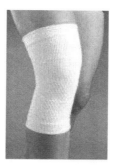

Elastic Knee Brace

I positioned the knee brace lower on my leg, so that it covered the area of my calf muscles. The Comfort Pad was placed between the elastic material and the skin, with the red-dot side facing outwards as always. This was very comfortable to wear, since the Comfort Pads had an exterior of cotton cloth, which absorbed sweat and made the pad "friendly" to the body. Frequently, I wore the brace + Comfort Pad arrangement during my sleep and woke up without any muscle stiffness, pain or cramping.

Here is an illustration of that method:

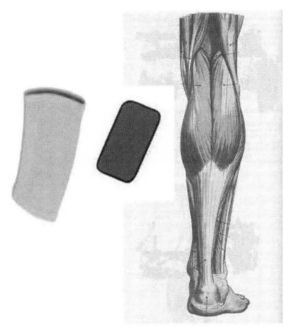

**Method: Place brace around calf, insert
Comfort Pad inside b r a c e**

TAPING MAGNETS TO SKIN:

As a second method, I tried simply taping super-magnets on top of the point of pain. After trying different arrangements, I found that 2 magnets taped to the upper part of the calf muscle worked best. Now, looking at the anatomical view of the calf muscles above, I can see why: there are 2 muscles involved, side by side.

Here's where I taped the magnets:

Alternate Treatment Method

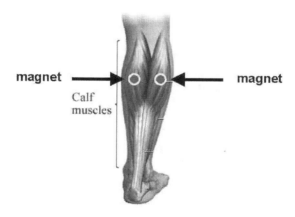

The results of the treatment

<u>Comfort Pad Method</u>: The use of the Comfort Pad always gave relief from the cramps within 10-30 minutes. When kept on for a longer time, the cramps did not return immediately; in generally, it was at

least a few days to a few weeks before they came again. Note that my Comfort Pads are extremely "loaded" with magnets: I have 2 layers, each with 11 magnets, for a total of 22 NdFeB super-magnets. They are also placed on 2 layers of magnetic rubber sheeting, of low magnetic strength. That's a lot of magnetic force!

Alternate Method – Taping Magnets: Surprisingly, taping 2 magnets to the skin above the muscles was as effective as the more generalized Comfort Pad. It was also more convenient, since one taping could be worn over a period of days (depending on the type of tape used and the sensitivity of the skin). In severe cases where the pain had to be stopped instantly, I used 2 magnets over each calf point as shown above.

Suggestions for general use

Using a Comfort Pad applies a more general magnetic field to the whole area and relaxes all the calf muscles. But when there is a point-specific problem, just taping magnets above that specific muscular point works fine. So if you haven't made your own ComfortPads, don't be discouraged.

And if you are going on a trip, for example, you can bring along 2 or 4 super-magnets and some tape. Then you'll be ready to handle acute muscular problems – cramps, pain, etc. – nearly anywhere on your body.

Knee Problems – Stretching Injury

The nature of the condition

During some over-strenuous exercise, I seriously damaged both my thigh muscles and the ligament attaching the thigh muscles to the kneecap. It was extremely painful when using the thigh muscles or flexing the knee. This pain continued for 18 months with little improvement before trying super-magnets.

Here are illustrations to help understand the muscles and tendons involved:

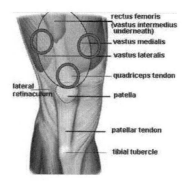

**Anatomy of front of leg, including
the knee and thigh**
(magnet placement shown by circles)

The light-colored oval shows where I had a stretching injury, causing significant pain. The orthopedic doctor told me that damage had been done to both the muscle (rectus femoris) and the quadriceps tendon that attaches it to the kneecap. Physiotherapy was prescribed, which only made it worse.

The magnetic treatment method

Here there were two different approaches used:

- For thigh-muscle pain, I used an elasticized thigh brace (slightly larger than a knee brace) and put a Comfort Pad underneath it and directly above the painful muscle.

- For acute pain from the tendon, which was felt under the kneecap, I taped2 super-magnets onto the skin. One was at the lower end of the muscle,one was at the "pocket" at the top of the knee, where the tendon joined tothe kneecap.

The results of the treatment

The large muscles had been having constant pain, somewhat like cramp pain. Each timeit happened, it stopped within a few minutes of applying the Comfort Pad over it.

The tendon / knee pain, much more acute, slowly improved over a period of 2-3 months.Since I also was taking a cartilage-improvement mineral supplement, it is impossible toknow the cause of the improvement. However, those supplements had beenpart of my diet before the injury, and it seems likely that the magnets over the damagedtendon were responsible – even if only partially – for the disappearance of the pain.

Suggestions for general use

Different magnetic therapy devices should be used where each is most e ffe c t i v e. Magnetic treatment methods should be different, depending on what kind of injury hashappened. The large-area Comfort Pads is best for large-muscle cramping, but it can stillhelp acute, localized pain – but a magnet or two, simply taped directly over a location ofacute pain, is often more effective and provides relief sooner.

Tennis elbow

The nature of the condition

What exactly is tennis elbow? The following information comes from Yahoo! Health, found at http://health.yahoo.com/ency/healthwise/hw225372 :

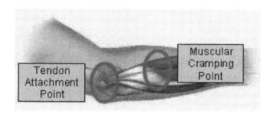

"Tennis elbow" is a term that describes soreness or pain on the outer (lateral) part of the elbow. While tennis elbow is common, playing tennis is only one of many activities that can result in this tendon injury. Also called lateral epicondylitis, tennis elbow occurs when there is tendon damage at the elbow where some of the forearm and hand muscles connect to the upper arm bone. It affects the muscles you use when extending your wrist and fingers.

This is a very painful situation and can come from carrying shopping bags and briefcases, as well as swinging a tennis racket. There are also similar painful conditions that result from muscle

Cramping in the upper forearm, as shown in the above diagram, sometimes even more painful than the tendon attachment point.

The usual home treatments include rest, ice, "counterforce braces" (see diagram below), elevation, aspirin-type (NSAIDS) medication, warm-up and stretching exercises. The counterforce brace, however, is mainly effective against muscular cramping although itdoes minimize stress on the tendon and lessens pain somewhat.

The magnetic treatment method

My experience says that there is another, more effective treatment: taping super-magnetsdirectly about the point(s) of pain. Overnight sleeping time is a convenient period f o r this. Counterforce braces are so common these days that you can wear one with magnetsinstalled and avoid curiosity-seekers until you have some answers for them. There are a number of magnetic tennis elbow braces on the market, similar to this d e s i g n :

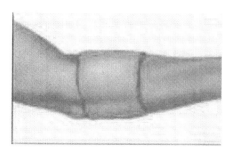

Typical Counterforce Brace

Do-It-Yourself Magnetic Therapy

Here's how to create your own custom "magnetic elbow brace":

- Purchase a tennis elbow elastic brace at a drugstore;
- Place it over the area that is painful;
- Place super-magnets inside the brace over the point of pain, with the red-dot side facing away from the body;
- Place another super-magnet on the outside of the brace. It will be attracted to the first magnet and will seat itself on the brace with the proper polarity.
- Now the 2 super-magnets are "locked" in place on the elastic brace.
- You can add more pairs of super-magnets for other points of pain.
- You can add more magnets on top of the ones you just installed – these will increase the power of the magnetic field on the selected painful point.
- I have found that a thickness of 2-3 super-magnets will improve nearly any muscular problem, including tennis elbow and others.

You can buy a basic wrap-around elbow brace at a drugstore or athletic supply store; you could also use an elastic "sweat band" that stretches enough to go around the arm.

Adding super-magnets will only take a moment; they can be ordered from the source listed in Appendix A for less than $1.00 apiece, plus shipping.

The most effective method for both tendon and muscular pain will look something likethe following illustration:

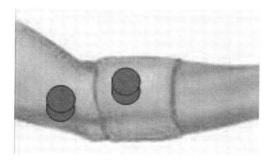

Here, the counterforce brace has a double layer of super-magnets:

- One inside and one outside the cloth material, keeping it fixed in place over muscles that are cramping or in serious pain; and

- A 2-stack of super-magnets taped about the "point of attachment" where the tendon and bone meet – the classical "tennis elbow" location.

The results of the treatment

My own tendon pain started improving immediately, and became close to normal withina few days of constant wear. The muscular pain near the elbow, resulting from closing the grip too strongly over long periods of time, was reduced immediately and in 2 days was almost completely gone.

Suggestions for general use

The long-term effect of the magnets depends a lot on your activities, of course. It also depends on the condition of your tendons and muscles – that is, whether they have been damaged, or whether they have a "habit" of remaining tense and causing themselves further pain. Magnets will remain effective as long as they are on the point of pain; if the magnets are removed and the pain returns, try them again. Naturally, if you don't have any relief from them, don't continue the treatment forever – there are many other approaches that are used (massage, liniment, acupuncture, whirlpool baths, etc.)

Foot pain due to flat feet / pronation

The nature of the condition

People with flat feet have little support when they walk, and it is tiring. Orthotics are custom-made insoles that provide needed support so that the body's weight is distributed properly. In essence, it provides an arch similar to that of an arched bridge, so that there is improved weight support.

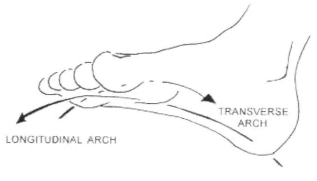

TRANSVERSE ARCH

LONGITUDINAL ARCH

Different arch supports: highway bridge, bottom of foot

Different people, of course, have different arch structures. Here is a comparison of 3 arch configurations:

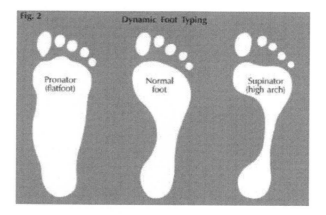

Especially with flat or pronated feet, even with arch supports in the shoes, foot muscles can still become tired, stressed or develop a muscular stress of tension "habit" from a lifetime of improper weight support. This is the area where super-magnets can be helpful – calming, relaxing and soothing these muscles so that a person can walk more normally. Note that super-magnets do not replace the function of Orthotics, but they can increase relaxation of the foot muscles and thereby decrease pain.

The magnetic treatment method

Here, we assume that the person suffers from flat feet and already has Orthotics in theirshoes. If not, they should make a small investment to get them – even the temporarymodels give good support.

The magnetic approach is as follows:

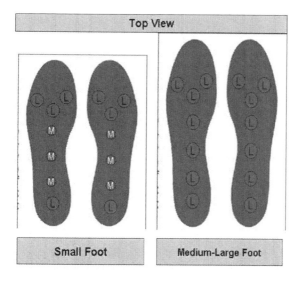

VIEW OF UNDER-SIDE OF INSOLE

Here, you are looking at the feet from a bottom-up point of view. The diagrams arelabeled backwards (right foot on the left side, etc.).   Why?

- The proper placement of the magnets is under the insole for maximum walking comfort;

- The red-dot labels MUST be facing away from the body, in this case down to the ground. So if we're seeing the magnets, we must be looking up from under the feet.

As shown above, there are 2 recommended super-magnet arrangements. One is for medium or large feet, and one for small feet:

- Use large magnets only (the red labels with an "L") at all positions indicated, since they are the most effective;

- Using large magnets at key points only, with medium-size magnets (the red labels with an "M") at intermediate points. This is because the magnets will repel each other and disturb the magnetic field if they are too close. If you feel that magnetic repulsion when placing magnets on your insole sheeting, you may wish to use the medium-size magnets along the length of the foot.

The second arrangement will be more comfortable for women with smaller feet.

What is the difference in this arrangement, compared with magnetic insoles on the market? Very simple: magnetic footpads on the market simply put magnets everywhere on the insole surface, creating a general magnetic field. The arrangement shown above places the strongest magnetic force under the 2 balls of the foot (large toe and small toe), under the acupuncture "kidney point" (between the balls of the feet) and under the "sleeping point" (at the heel) – all as suggested by Traditional Chinese Medicine. You will find that these locations fit well with a map of the meridians of the body, which terminate at the sole of the foot.

You may also have specific health problems that suggest additional magnet locations. This would mean consulting a doctor in Oriental Medicine or a Reflexologist. However, the magnet location points in the chart above are a good start, since they focus on major muscular stress points in the foot.

The results of the treatment

I have found that my Orthotics feel much more comfortable when there are magnets underneath. Others with foot problems have reported the same results.

What is most interesting is that people with no foot problems at all have also found themagnetic footpads helpful. They report that they feel "lighter on their feet".

Suggestions for general use

These magnetic insoles are simple to make and cost little money. The major investmentis the magnetic sheet material to which they are fixed. If you don't have enough moneyto purchase a minimum-size 10-foot role (about $35), you could glue the magnets to a standard drugstore insole pad. It will be less effective, but should still provide some relief from pain.

Our thanks for your buying this book

We hope that this book has given you valuable information. Trust yourself to make these magnetic devices and test them. If you use true neodymium magnets of about 10,000 gauss strength, I believe you will be pleased with the results.

Appendix A – Purchase Resources

Purchasing Neodymium magnets

I dealt with a number of companies with magnetic products. The best I found, from a price and quality of service perspective, was All Magnetics in California.

The company's URL is www.allmagnetics.com, and the specific page to look at is http://www.allmagnetics.com/neodymium.htm. Their packaged magnets show a force of 10,000 Gauss, but the ones they sent me had a force of 12,500 Gauss (industrial strength, literally). I recommend you call the 1-800-262-4638 telephone number. I found the disc about the size of a quarter to be the best-working.

Special tip: taping a pair of these magnets directly above the point of pain (very tight magnetic field for muscles, joints, etc.) is often more effective than applying a large pad (more general, large magnetic field). Of course, make sure that the red-labeled side is pointing away from the body for best results.

You may not need to construct any pads at all, depending on your results with the taped magnet-pairs. And use them wherever there is pain or discomfort - be an experimenter. You'll find that the magnets have an amazing breadth of application.

Suggestions re magnetic backing sheet

From the above supplier, flexible magnetic sheeting is only available in rolls. My experience is that you can sometimes obtain smaller sizes at a local print shop, since this sheeting is used for magnetic refrigerator stick-on business cards. Also, if memory serves, it is best to get the .030" thickness sheet. Thinner sheets do not provide enough stiffness, and thicker sheets are not sufficiently flexible.

Made in the USA
Middletown, DE
21 June 2024

56137300R00045